CHRIST AND CHRISTMAS

CHRIST AND CHRISTMAS

A Poem

BY

MARY BAKER EDDY

DISCOVERER AND FOUNDER OF CHRISTIAN SCIENCE
AND AUTHOR OF SCIENCE AND HEALTH WITH
KEY TO THE SCRIPTURES

Published by the
Trustees under the Will of Mary Baker G. Eddy
BOSTON, U.S.A.

CHRIST AND CHRISTMAS

CHRIST AND CHRISTMAS

FAST circling on, from zone to zone, —
    Bright, blest, afar, —
O'er the grim night of chaos shone
    One lone, brave star.

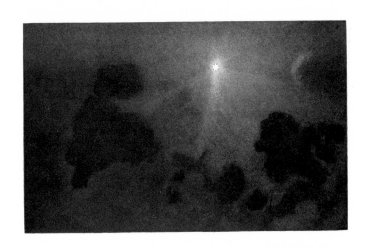

STAR OF BETHLEHEM

O'er the grim night of chaos shone
One lone, brave star.

[9]

IN tender mercy, Spirit sped
    A loyal ray
To rouse the living, wake the dead,
    And point the Way —

The Christ-idea, God anoints —
    Of Truth and Life;
The Way in Science He appoints,
    That stills all strife.

CHRIST HEALING

The Way in Science He appoints,
That stills all strife.

WHAT the Beloved knew and taught,
  Science repeats,
Through understanding, dearly sought,
  With fierce heart-beats;

SEEKING AND FINDING

Through understanding, dearly sought,
With fierce heart-beats;

THUS Christ, eternal and divine,
 To celebrate
As Truth demands, — this living Vine
 Ye demonstrate.

For heaven's CHRISTUS, earthly Eves,
 By Adam bid,
Make merriment on Christmas eves,
 O'er babe and crib.

CHRISTMAS EVE

Make merriment on Christmas eves,
O'er babe and crib.

YET wherefore signalize the birth
    Of him ne'er born?
What can rehearse the glorious worth
    Of his high morn?

CHRISTMAS MORN

What can rehearse the glorious worth
  Of his high morn?

CHRIST was not crucified — that doom
  Was Jesus' part;
For Sharon's rose must bud and bloom
  In human heart.*

Forever present, bounteous, free,
  Christ comes in gloom;
And aye, with grace towards you and me,
  For health makes room.

  * "God was manifest in the flesh."— *St. Paul.*

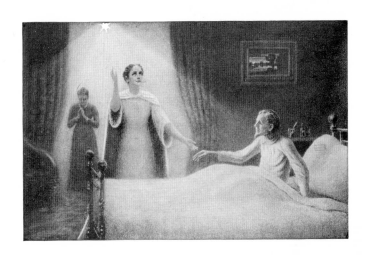

CHRISTIAN SCIENCE HEALING

And aye, with grace towards you and me,
For health makes room.

THUS olden faith's pale star now blends
    In seven-hued white!
Life, without birth and without end,
    Emitting light!

I THANK THEE, O FATHER, LORD OF HEAVEN AND EARTH, BECAUSE
THOU HAST HID THESE THINGS FROM THE WISE AND PRUDENT, AND
HAST REVEALED THEM UNTO BABES. — *Christ Jesus*

Life, without birth and without end,
Emitting light !

THE Way, the Truth, the Life — His word —
    Are here, and now
Christ's silent healing, heaven heard,
    Crowns the pale brow.

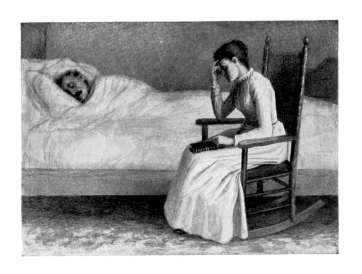

TREATING THE SICK

Christ's silent healing, heaven heard,
Crowns the pale brow.

FOR Christian Science brings to view
    The great I Am, —
Omniscient power, — gleaming through
    Mind, mother, man.

As in blest Palestina's hour,
    So in our age,
'T is the same hand unfolds His power,
    And writes the page.

CHRISTIAN UNITY

'T is the same hand unfolds His power,
  And writes the page.

[41]

To-DAY, as oft, away from sin
    Christ summons thee!
Truth pleads to-night: Just take Me in!
    No mass for Me!

TRUTH *VERSUS* ERROR

Truth pleads to-night: Just take Me in!
No mass for Me!

NO blight, no broken wing, no moan,
  Truth's fane can dim;
Eternal swells Christ's music-tone,
  In heaven's hymn.

THE WAY

Eternal swells Christ's music-tone,
In heaven's hymn.

[49]

POEM AND GLOSSARY

CHRIST AND CHRISTMAS

1. Fast circling on, from zone to zone,—
   Bright, blest, afar,—
   O'er the grim night of chaos shone
   One lone, brave star.

2. In tender mercy, Spirit sped
   A loyal ray
   To rouse the living, wake the dead,
   And point the Way—

3. The Christ-idea, God anoints—
   Of Truth and Life;
   The Way in Science He appoints,
   That stills all strife.

4. What the Beloved knew and taught,
   Science repeats,
   Through understanding, dearly sought,
   With fierce heart-beats;

5. Thus Christ, eternal and divine,
   To celebrate
   As Truth demands,—this living Vine
   Ye demonstrate.

6. For heaven's *Christus*, earthly Eves,
   By Adam bid,
   Make merriment on Christmas eves,
   O'er babe and crib.

7. Yet wherefore signalize the birth
   Of him ne'er born?
   What can rehearse the glorious worth
   Of his high morn?

8. Christ was not crucified—that doom
   Was Jesus' part;
   For Sharon's rose must bud and bloom
   In human heart.°

9. Forever present, bounteous, free,
   Christ comes in gloom;
   And aye, with grace towards you and me,
   For health makes room.

10. Thus olden faith's pale star now blends
    In seven-hued white!
    Life, without birth and without end,
    Emitting light!

11. The Way, the Truth, the Life—His word—
    Are here, and now
    Christ's silent healing, heaven heard,
    Crowns the pale brow.

12. For Christian Science brings to view
    The great I Am,—
    Omniscient power,—gleaming through
    Mind, mother, man.

13. As in blest Palestina's hour,
    So in our age,
    'T is the same hand unfolds His power,
    And writes the page.

14. To-day, as oft, away from sin
    Christ summons thee!
    Truth pleads to-night: Just take Me in!
    No mass for Me!

15. No blight, no broken wing, no moan,
    Truth's fane can dim;
    Eternal swells Christ's music-tone,
    In heaven's hymn.

°"God was manifest in the flesh."—*St. Paul.*

GLOSSARY

These Scriptural texts are the basis of the sentiments in the verses, whereto
their number corresponds.

VERSE

1. I am the root and the offspring of David, and the bright and morning star. — *Christ Jesus.*

2. Verily, verily, I say unto you, The hour is coming, and now is, when the dead shall hear the voice of the Son of God: and they that hear shall live. — *Christ Jesus.*

3. The people that walked in darkness have seen a great light: they that dwell in the land of the shadow of death, upon them hath the light shined. — *Isaiah.*

4. But seek ye first the kingdom of God, and His righteousness; and all these things shall be added unto you. — *Christ Jesus.*

5. The tabret, and pipe, and wine, are in their feasts: but they regard not the work of the Lord, neither consider the operation of His hands. — *Isaiah.*

6. Man that is born of a woman is of few days, and full of trouble.
— *Job.*

7. Before Abraham was, I am. — *Christ Jesus.*

8. If Christ be in you, the body is dead because of sin; but the Spirit [God-likeness] is life because of righteousness.
— *St. Paul.*

9. But such as I have give I thee: In the name of Jesus Christ of Nazareth rise up and walk. — *St. Peter.*

10. Without father, without mother, without descent, having neither beginning of days, nor end of life; but made like unto the Son of God. — *St. Paul.*

11. Heal the sick. — *Christ Jesus.*

12. For whosoever shall do the will of my Father which is in heaven, the same is my brother, and sister, and mother.
— *Christ Jesus.*

13. And there shall be one fold, and one shepherd. — *Christ Jesus.*

14. Behold, I stand at the door, and knock: if any man hear my voice, and open the door, I will come in to him, and will sup with him, and he with me. — *Christ Jesus.*

15. And whosoever liveth and believeth in me shall never die.
— *Christ Jesus.*

AND he that overcometh, and keepeth my works unto the end, to him will I give power over the nations:

And I will give him the MORNING STAR.

— *Christ Jesus*

MARY BAKER EDDY
AND
JAMES F. GILMAN
ARTISTS

POEMS

POEMS

BY

MARY BAKER EDDY

DISCOVERER AND FOUNDER OF CHRISTIAN SCIENCE
AND AUTHOR OF SCIENCE AND HEALTH WITH
KEY TO THE SCRIPTURES

Published by the
Trustees under the Will
of Mary Baker G. Eddy
BOSTON, U. S. A.

Authorized Literature of
THE FIRST CHURCH OF CHRIST, SCIENTIST
in Boston, Massachusetts

PREFACE

The poems garnered up in this little volume were written at different periods in the life of the author, dating from her early girlhood up to recent years. They were not written with a view of making a book, each poem being the spontaneous outpouring of a deeply poetic nature and called forth by some experience that claimed her attention.

The "Old Man of the Mountain," for instance, was written while the author was contemplating this lofty New Hampshire crag, whose rugged outlines resemble the profile of a human face. Inspired by the grandeur of this masterpiece of nature's handiwork, and looking "up through nature, unto nature's God," the poem began to take form in her thought, and alighting from her carriage, she seated herself by the roadside and began to write. Some tourists who were passing, and who made her acquaintance, asked her what she was writing, and she replied by reading the poem to them. They were so pleased with it that each requested a copy, which was subsequently mailed to them. Similar requests continued to reach the author for years afterward, until the poem finally found its way into print, appearing, together with " The Valley Cemetery," in a book " Gems for You," published in Manchester, N. H., in 1850, and again in Boston, in 1856.

The poem on the " Dedication of a Temperance Hall," in Lynn, Mass., in 1866, was written for that occasion, and was sung by the audience as a dedicatory hymn. " The Liberty Bells " appeared in a Lynn, Mass., newspaper, under the date of February 3, 1865. A note from the author, which was published with the poem, read as follows:

" MR. EDITOR: — In 1835 a mob in Boston (although Boston has since been the pioneer of anti-slavery) dispersed a meeting of the Female Anti-Slavery Society, and assailed the person of William Lloyd Garrison with such fury that the city authorities could protect him nowhere but in the walls of a jail. To-day, by order of Governor Andrew, the bells are ringing to celebrate the passing of a resolution in Congress prohibiting slavery in the United States."

All of the author's best-known hymns are included in this collection, as well as many poems written in girlhood and during the years she resided in Lynn, Mass., and which appeared in various publications of that day. Among her earliest poems are " Upward," " Resolutions for the Day," " Autumn " (written in a maple grove), " Alpha-

bet and Bayonet," and " The Country-Seat " (written while visiting a family friend in the beautiful
suburbs of Boston); yet, even these are characterized
by the same lofty trend of thought that reached its
fullness in her later productions.

In May, 1910, Mrs. Eddy requested her pub-
lisher to prepare a few bound volumes of her poems,
for private distribution. When this became known
to her friends, they urged her to allow a popular
edition to be issued, to which she assented. With
grateful acknowledgment, therefore, of this per-
mission, this little volume is presented to the public,
in the hope that these gems of purest thought
from this spiritually-minded author will prove
a joy to the heavy laden and a balm to the weary
heart.

ADAM H. DICKEY

CHESTNUT HILL, MASS., September 24, 1910

CONTENTS

POEMS

Poems

OLD MAN OF THE MOUNTAIN

Gigantic sire, unfallen still thy
    crest!
Primeval dweller where the wild winds
    rest,
Beyond the ken of mortal e'er to tell
What power sustains thee in thy rock-bound
    cell.

Or if, when first creation vast began,
And far the universal fiat ran,
"Let there be light" — from chaos dark set
    free,
Ye rose, a monument of Deity,

Proud from yon cloud-crowned height to
    look henceforth
On insignificance that peoples earth,
Recalling oft the bitter draft which turns
The mind to meditate on what it learns.

Stern, passionless, no soul those looks betray;
Though kindred rocks, to sport at mortal
    clay —
Much as the chisel of the sculptor's art
" Plays round the head, but comes not to
    the heart."

Ah, who can fathom thee!   Ambitious man,
Like a trained falcon in the Gallic van,
Guided and led, can never reach to thee
With all the strength of weakness — vanity!

Great as thou art, and paralleled by none,
Admired by all, still art thou drear and lone!
The moon looks down upon thine exiled
    height;
The stars, so cold, so glitteringly bright,

On wings of morning gladly flit away,
Yield to the sun's more genial, mighty ray;
The white waves kiss the murmuring rill —
But thy deep silence is unbroken still.

CONSTANCY

When starlight blends with morn-
ing's hue,
I miss thee as the flower the dew!
When noonday's length'ning shad-
ows flee,
I think of thee, I think of thee!

With evening, memories reappear —
I watch thy chair, and wish thee here;
Till sleep sets drooping fancy free
To dream of thee, to dream of thee!

Since first we met, in weal or woe
It hath been thus; and must be so
Till bursting bonds our spirits part
And Love divine doth fill my heart.

Written many years ago

THE MOTHER'S EVENING PRAYER

O GENTLE presence, peace and joy
   and power;
  O Life divine, that owns each
    waiting hour,
Thou Love that guards the nestling's falter-
   ing flight!
  Keep Thou my child on upward wing
    tonight.

Love is our refuge; only with mine eye
  Can I behold the snare, the pit, the fall:
His habitation high is here, and nigh,
   His arm encircles me, and mine, and all.

O make me glad for every scalding tear,
  For hope deferred, ingratitude, disdain!
Wait, and love more for every hate, and fear
   No ill, — since God is good, and loss is gain.

Beneath the shadow of His mighty wing;
  In that sweet secret of the narrow way,
Seeking and finding, with the angels sing:
   "Lo, I am with you alway," — watch and
    pray.

No snare, no fowler, pestilence or pain;
  No night drops down upon the troubled
    breast,
When heaven's aftersmile earth's tear-drops
    gain,
  And mother finds her home and heav'nly
    rest.

LOVE

Brood o'er us with Thy shelt'ring
      wing,
   'Neath which our spirits blend
Like brother birds, that soar and
      sing,
   And on the same branch bend.
The arrow that doth wound the dove
Darts not from those who watch and love.

If thou the bending reed wouldst break
   By thought or word unkind,
Pray that his spirit you partake,
   Who loved and healed mankind:
Seek holy thoughts and heavenly strain,
That make men one in love remain.

Learn, too, that wisdom's rod is given
   For faith to kiss, and know;
That greetings glorious from high heaven,
   Whence joys supernal flow,
Come from that Love, divinely near,
Which chastens pride and earth-born fear,

Through God, who gave that word of might
   Which swelled creation's lay:
" Let there be light, and there was light."
   What chased the clouds away?
'Twas Love whose finger traced aloud
A bow of promise on the cloud.

Thou to whose power our hope we give,
   Free us from human strife.
Fed by Thy love divine we live,
   For Love alone is Life;
And life most sweet, as heart to heart
Speaks kindly when we meet and part.

I'M SITTING ALONE

I'M sitting alone where the shadows
    fall
In somber groups at the vesper-call,
Where tear-dews of night seek the
        loving rose,
Her bosom to fill with mortal woes.

I'm waiting alone for the bridal hour
Of nymph and naiad from woodland bower;
Till vestal pearls that on leaflets lay,
Ravished with beauty the eye of day.

I'm watching alone o'er the starlit glow,
O'er the silv'ry moon and ocean flow;
And sketching in light the heaven of my
        youth —
Its starry hopes and its waves of truth.

I'm dreaming alone of its changeful sky —
What rainbows of rapture floated by!
Of a mother's love, that no words could speak
When parting the ringlets to kiss my cheek.

I'm thinking alone of a fair young bride,
The light of a home of love and pride;

How the glance of her husband's watchful eye
Turned to his star of idolatry.

I'm picturing alone a glad young face,
Upturned to his mother's in playful grace;
And the unsealed fountains of grief and joy
That gushed at the birth of that beautiful
    boy.

I'm weeping alone that the vision is fled,
The leaves all faded, the fruitage shed,
And wishing this earth more gifts from above,
Our reason made right and hearts all love.

LYNN, MASS., September 3, 1866

THE UNITED STATES TO
GREAT BRITAIN

Hail, brother! fling thy banner
  To the billows and the breeze;
We proffer thee warm welcome
  With our hand, though not
    our knees.

Lord of the main and manor!
  Thy palm, in ancient day,
Didst rock the country's cradle
  That wakes thy laureate's lay.

The hoar fight is forgotten;
  Our eagle, like the dove,
Returns to bless a bridal
  Betokened from above.

List, brother! angels whisper
  To Judah's sceptered race, —
"Thou of the self-same spirit,
  Allied by nations' grace,

"Wouldst cheer the hosts of heaven;
  For Anglo-Israel, lo!
Is marching under orders;
  His hand averts the blow."

Brave Britain, blest America!
  Unite your battle-plan;
Victorious, all who live it, —
  The love for God and man.

Boston Herald, Sunday, May 15, 1898

CHRIST MY REFUGE

O'ER waiting harpstrings of the mind
    There sweeps a strain,
Low, sad, and sweet, whose meas-
        ures bind
    The power of pain,

And wake a white-winged angel throng
    Of thoughts, illumed
By faith, and breathed in raptured song,
    With love perfumed.

Then His unveiled, sweet mercies show
    Life's burdens light.
I kiss the cross, and wake to know
    A world more bright.

And o'er earth's troubled, angry sea
    I see Christ walk,
And come to me, and tenderly,
    Divinely talk.

Thus Truth engrounds me on the rock,
    Upon Life's shore,
'Gainst which the winds and waves can
        shock,
    Oh, nevermore!

From tired joy and grief afar,
    And nearer Thee, —
Father, where Thine own children are,
    I love to be.

My prayer, some daily good to do
    To Thine, for Thee;
An offering pure of Love, whereto
    God leadeth me.

"FEED MY SHEEP"

SHEPHERD, show me how to go
   O'er the hillside steep,
How to gather, how to sow, —
   How to feed Thy sheep;
I will listen for Thy voice,
   Lest my footsteps stray;
I will follow and rejoice
   All the rugged way.

Thou wilt bind the stubborn will,
   Wound the callous breast,
Make self-righteousness be still,
   Break earth's stupid rest.
Strangers on a barren shore,
   Lab'ring long and lone,
We would enter by the door,
   And Thou know'st Thine own;

So, when day grows dark and cold,
   Tear or triumph harms,
Lead Thy lambkins to the fold,
   Take them in Thine arms;
Feed the hungry, heal the heart,
   Till the morning's beam;
White as wool, ere they depart,
   Shepherd, wash them clean.

THE VALLEY CEMETERY

Ye soft sighing zephyrs through foli-
    age and vine!
Ye echoing moans from the foot-
    steps of time!
Break not on the silence, unless thou canst
    bear
A message from heaven — " No partings are
    there."

Here gloom hath enchantment in beauty's
    array,
And whispering voices are calling away —
Their wooings are soft as the vision more
    vain —
I would live in their empire, or die in their
    chain.

Here smileth the blossom and sunshine not
    dead —
Flowers fresh as the pang in the bosom that
    bled, —
Yes, constant as love that outliveth the
    grave,
And time cannot quench in oblivion's wave.

And thou, gentle cypress, in evergreen tears,
Art constant and hopeful though winter
    appears.
My heart hath thy verdure, it blossoms
    above;
Like thee, it endureth and liveth in love.

Ambition, come hither! These vaults will
    unfold
The sequel of power, of glory, or gold;
Then rush into life, and roll on with its tide,
And bustle and toil for its pomp and its pride.

The tired wings flitting through far crimson
    glow,
Which steepeth the trees when the day-god
    is low;
The voice of the night-bird must here send a
    thrill
To the heart of the leaves when the winds
    are all still.

'Mid graves do I hear the glad voices that
    swell,
And call to my spirit with seraphs to dwell;
They come with a breath from the verdant
    springtime,
And waken my joy, as in earliest prime.

Blest beings departed! Ye echoes at dawn!
O tell of their radiant home and its morn!
Then I'll think of its glory, and rest till I see
My loved ones in glory still waiting for me.

UPWARD

I'VE watched in the azure the eagle's
        proud wing,
His soaring majestic, and feather-
        some fling —
Careening in liberty higher and higher —
Like genius unfolding a quenchless desire.

Would a tear dim his eye, or pinion lose
        power
To gaze on the lark in her emerald bower?
When higher he soareth to compass his rest,
What vision so bright as the dream in his
        breast!

God's eye is upon him. He penciled his
        path
Whose omniscient notice the frail fledgling
        hath.
Though lightnings be lurid and earthquakes
        may shock,
He rides on the whirlwind or rests on the
        rock.

My course, like the eagle's, oh, still be it high,
Celestial the breezes that waft o'er its sky!
God's eye is upon me — I am not alone
When onward and upward and heavenward
          borne.

Written in early years

THE OAK ON THE MOUNTAIN'S SUMMIT

O<small>H</small>, mountain monarch, at whose
    feet I stand, —
Clouds to adorn thy brow, skies
    clasp thy hand, —
Nature divine, in harmony profound,
With peaceful presence hath begirt thee
    round.

And thou, majestic oak, from yon high place
Guard'st thou the earth, asleep in night's
    embrace, —
And from thy lofty summit, pouring down
Thy sheltering shade, her noonday glories
    crown?

Whate'er thy mission, mountain sentinel,
To my lone heart thou art a power and spell;
A lesson grave, of life, that teacheth me
To love the Hebrew figure of a tree.

Faithful and patient be my life as thine;
As strong to wrestle with the storms of time;
As deeply rooted in a soil of love;
As grandly rising to the heavens above.

WOMAN'S RIGHTS

G_RAVE_ on her monumental pile:
She won from vice, by virtue's
    smile,
Her dazzling crown, her sceptered
    throne,
Affection's wreath, a happy home;

The right to worship deep and pure,
To bless the orphan, feed the poor;
Last at the cross to mourn her Lord,
First at the tomb to hear his word:

To fold an angel's wings below;
And hover o'er the couch of woe;
To nurse the Bethlehem babe so sweet,
The right to sit at Jesus' feet;

To form the bud for bursting bloom,
The hoary head with joy to crown;
In short, the right to work and pray,
" To point to heaven and lead the way."

LYNN, MASS., May 6, 1876

THE NEW CENTURY

T HOU God-crowned, patient century,
Thine hour hath come! Eternity
Draws nigh — and, beckoning from
 above,
One hundred years, aflame with Love,
Again shall bid old earth good-by —
And, lo, the light! far heaven is nigh!
New themes seraphic, Life divine,
And bliss that wipes the tears of time
Away, will enter, when they may,
And bask in one eternal day.

'Tis writ on earth, on leaf and flower:
Love hath one race, one realm, one power.
Dear God! how great, how good Thou art
To heal humanity's sore heart;
To probe the wound, then pour the balm —
A life perfected, strong and calm.
The dark domain of pain and sin
Surrenders — Love doth enter in,
And peace is won, and lost is vice:
Right reigns, and blood was not its price.

PLEASANT VIEW, CONCORD, N. H., January, 1901

TO MY ABSENT BROTHER

Dwells there a shadow on thy
     brow —
  A look that years impart?
Does there a thought of van-
     ished hours
  Come ever o'er thy heart?

Or give those earnest eyes yet back
  An image of the soul,
Mirrored in truth, in light and joy,
  Above the world's control?

So may their gaze be ever fraught
  With utterance deep and strong,
Yielding a holy strength to right,
  A stern rebuke to wrong!

Thy soul, upborne on wisdom's wings,
  In brighter morn will find
Life hath a higher recompense
  Than just to please mankind.

Supreme and omnipresent God,
  Guide him in wisdom's way!
Give peaceful triumph to the truth,
  Bid error melt away!

LYNN, MASS., November 8, 1866

SIGNS OF THE HEART

Come to me, joys of heaven!
  Breathe through the summer air
A balm — the long-lost leaven
  Dissolving death, despair!
    O little heart,
    To me thou art
A sign that never can depart.

Come to me, peace on earth!
  From out life's billowy sea, —
A wave of welcome birth, —
  The Life that lives in Thee!
    O Love divine,
    This heart of Thine
Is all I need to comfort mine.

Come when the shadows fall,
  And night grows deeply dark;
The barren brood, O call
  With song of morning lark;
    And from above,
    Dear heart of Love,
Send us thy white-winged dove.

PLEASANT VIEW, CONCORD, N. H., 1899

FLOWERS

Mirrors of morn
Whence the dewdrop is born,
Soft tints of the rainbow and
  skies —
Sisters of song,
What a shadowy throng
Around you in memory rise!

Far do ye flee,
From your green bowers free,
Fair floral apostles of love,
Sweetly to shed
Fragrance fresh round the dead,
And breath of the living above.

Flowers for the brave —
Be he monarch or slave,
Whose heart bore its grief and is still!
Flowers for the kind —
Aye, the Christians who wind
Wreaths for the triumphs o'er ill!

PLEASANT VIEW, CONCORD, N. H., May 21, 1904

TO THE OLD YEAR — 1865

P<small>ASS</small> on, returnless year!
The track behind thee is with
    glory crowned;
The turf where thou hast trod is
    holy ground.
    Pass proudly to thy bier!

    Chill was thy midnight day,
While Justice grasped the sword to hold her
    throne,
And on her altar our loved Lincoln's own
    Great willing heart did lay.

    Thy purpose hath been won!
Thou point'st thy phantom finger, grim and
    cold,
To the dark record of our guilt unrolled,
    And smiling, say'st, " 'Tis done!

    " This record I will bear
To the dim chambers of eternity —
The chain and charter I have lived to see
    Purged by the cannon's prayer;

"Convulsion, carnage, war;
The pomp and tinsel of unrighteous power;
Bloated oppression in its awful hour, —
    I, dying, dare abhor!"

    One word, receding year,
Ere thou grow tremulous with shadowy
        night!
Say, will the young year dawn with wisdom's
        light
    To brighten o'er thy bier?

    Or we the past forget,
And heal her wounds too tenderly to last?
Or let today grow difficult and vast
    With traitors unvoiced yet?

    Though thou must leave the tear, —
Hearts bleeding ere they break in silence yet,
Wrong jubilant and right with bright eye
        wet, —
    Thou fast expiring year,

    Thy work is done, and well:
Thou hast borne burdens, and may take thy
        rest,
Pillow thy head on time's untired breast.
    Illustrious year, farewell!

Lynn, Mass., January 1, 1866

INVOCATION FOR 1868

Father of every age,
  Of every rolling sphere,
Help us to write a death-
    less page
    Of truth, this dawning year!

Help us to humbly bow
  To Thy all-wise behest —
Whate'er the gift of joy or woe,
  Knowing Thou knowest best.

Aid our poor soul to sing
  Above the tempest's glee;
Give us the eagle's fearless wing,
  The dove's to soar to Thee!

All-merciful and good,
  Hover the homeless heart!
Give us this day our daily food
  In knowing what Thou art!

SWAMPSCOTT, MASS., January 1, 1868

CHRISTMAS MORN

Blest Christmas morn, though
    murky clouds
  Pursue thy way,
Thy light was born where storm
    enshrouds
  Nor dawn nor day!

Dear Christ, forever here and near,
  No cradle song,
No natal hour and mother's tear,
  To thee belong.

Thou God-idea, Life-encrowned,
  The Bethlehem babe —
Beloved, replete, by flesh embound —
  Was but thy shade!

Thou gentle beam of living Love,
  And deathless Life!
Truth infinite, — so far above
  All mortal strife,

Or cruel creed, or earth-born taint:
  Fill us today
With all thou art — be thou our saint,
  Our stay, alway.

December, 1898

EASTER MORN

Gently thou beckonest from the
    giant hills
The new-born beauty in the emer-
    ald sky,
And wakening murmurs from the drowsy
    rills —
  O gladsome dayspring! 'reft of mortal sigh
To glorify all time — eternity —
With thy still fathomless Christ-majesty.

E'en as Thou gildest gladdened joy, dear
    God,
  Give risen power to prayer; fan Thou the
    flame
Of right with might; and midst the rod,
  And stern, dark shadows cast on Thy blest
    name,
Lift Thou a patient love above earth's ire,
Piercing the clouds with its triumphal spire.

While sacred song and loudest breath of
    praise
  Echo amid the hymning spheres of light, —
With heaven's lyres and angel's loving lays, —

Send to the loyal struggler for the right,
Joy — not of time, nor yet by nature sown,
But the celestial seed dropped from Love's
    throne.

Prolong the strain "Christ risen!" Sad sense,
    annoy
  No more the peace of Soul's sweet solitude!
Deep loneness, tear-filled tones of distant joy,
  Depart! Glad Easter glows with grati-
    tude —
Love's verdure veils the leaflet's wondrous
    birth —
Rich rays, rare footprints on the dust of earth.

Not life, the vassal of the changeful hour,
  Nor burdened bliss, but Truth and Love
    attest
The solemn splendor of immortal power, —
  The ever Christ, and glorified behest,
Poured on the sense which deems no suffering
    vain
That wipes away the sting of death — sin,
  pain.

PLEASANT VIEW, CONCORD, N. H., April 18, 1900

RESOLUTIONS FOR THE DAY

To rise in the morning and drink in
    the view —
  The home where I dwell in the
    vale,
The blossoms whose fragrance and charms
    ever new
  Are scattered o'er hillside and dale;

To gaze on the sunbeams enkindling the
    sky —
  A loftier life to invite —
A light that illumines my spiritual eye,
  And inspires my pen as I write;

To form resolutions, with strength from on
    high,
  Such physical laws to obey,
As reason with appetite, pleasures deny,
  That health may my efforts repay;

To kneel at the altar of mercy and pray
  That pardon and grace, through His Son,
May comfort my soul all the wearisome day,
  And cheer me with hope when 'tis done;

To daily remember my blessings and charge,
  And make this my humble request:
Increase Thou my faith and my vision
    enlarge,
  And bless me with Christ's promised rest;

To hourly seek for deliverance strong
  From selfishness, sinfulness, dearth,
From vanity, folly, and all that is wrong —
  With ambition that binds us to earth;

To kindly pass over a wound, or a foe
  (And mem'ry but part us awhile),
To breathe forth a prayer that His love I
    may know,
  Whose mercies my sorrows beguile, —

If these resolutions are acted up to,
  And faith spreads her pinions abroad,
'Twill be sweet when I ponder the days may
    be few
  That waft me away to my God.

Written in girlhood

O FOR THY WINGS, SWEET BIRD!

O FOR thy wings, sweet bird!
  And soul of melody by being
    blest —
Like thee, my voice had stirred
  Some dear remembrance in a weary breast.

But whither wouldst thou rove,
  Bird of the airy wing, and fold thy plumes?
In what dark leafy grove
  Wouldst chant thy vespers 'mid rich
    glooms?

Or sing thy love-lorn note —
  In deeper solitude, where nymph or saint
Has wooed some mystic spot,
  Divinely desolate the shrine to paint?

Yet wherefore ask thy doom?
  Blessed compared with me thou art —
Unto thy greenwood home
  Bearing no bitter memory at heart;

Wearing no earthly chain,
  Thou canst in azure bright soar far above;
Nor pinest thou in vain
  O'er joys departed, unforgotten love.

O take me to thy bower!
  Beguile the lagging hours of weariness
With strain which hath strange power
  To make me love thee as I love life less!

From mortal consciousness
  Which binds to earth — infirmity of woe!
Or pining tenderness —
  Whose streams will never dry or cease to
    flow;

An aching, voiceless void,
  Hushed in the heart whereunto none reply,
And in the cringing crowd
  Companionless! Bird, bear me through
    the sky!

Written more than eighty years ago
for the *New Hampshire Patriot*

COME THOU

Come, in the minstrel's lay;
 When two hearts meet,
 And true hearts greet,
And all is morn and May.

Come Thou! and now, anew,
 To thought and deed
 Give sober speed,
Thy will to know, and do.

Stay! till the storms are o'er —
 The cold blasts done,
 The reign of heaven begun,
And Love, the evermore.

Be patient, waiting heart:
 Light, Love divine
 Is here, and thine;
You therefore cannot part.

" The seasons come and go:
 Love, like the sea,
 Rolls on with thee, —
But knows no ebb and flow.

" Faith, hope, and tears, triune,
 Above the sod
 Find peace in God,
And one eternal noon."

Oh, Thou hast heard my prayer;
 And I am blest!
 This is Thy high behest:
Thou, here and *everywhere*.

WISH AND ITEM

To the editor of the *Item*, Lynn, Mass.

I HOPE the heart that's hungry
  For things above the floor,
Will find within its portals
  An item rich in store;

That melancholy mortals
  Will count their mercies o'er,
And learn that Truth and wisdom
  Have many items more;

That when a wrong is done us,
  It stirs no thought of strife;
And Love becomes the substance,
  As item, of our life;

That every ragged urchin,
  With bare feet soiled or sore,
Share God's most tender mercies, —
  Find items at our door.

Then if we've done to others
  Some good ne'er told before,
When angels shall repeat it,
  'Twill be an item more.

DEDICATION OF A TEMPERANCE HALL

AUTHOR of all divine
  Gifts, lofty, pure, and free,
Temperance and truth in song
    sublime
  An offering bring to Thee!

A temple, whose high dome
  Rose from a water-cup;
And from its altar to Thy throne
  May we press on and up!

And she — last at the cross,
  First at the tomb, who waits —
Woman — will watch to cleanse from dross
  The cause she elevates.

Sons of the old Bay State,
  Work for our glorious cause!
And be your waiting hearts elate,
  Since temperance makes your laws.

" Temples of Honor," all,
  " Social," or grand, or great,
This blazoned, brilliant temperance hall
  To Thee we dedicate.

" Good Templars " one and all,
  Good " Sons," and daughters, too,
We dedicate this temperance hall
  To God, to Truth, and you!

LYNN, MASS., August 4, 1866

LINES

Come, rest in this bosom, my own stricken deer
— Moore

Was that fold for the lambkin soft
    virtue's repose,
Where the weary and earth-
    stricken lay down their woes, —
When the fountain and leaflet are frozen and
    sere,
And the mountains more friendless, — their
    home is not here?

When the herd had forsaken, and left them
    to stray
From the green sunny slopes of the woodland
    away;
Where the music of waters had fled to the sea,
And this life but one given to suffer and be?

Was it then thou didst call them to banish
    all pain,
And the harpstring, just breaking, reecho
    again
To a strain of enchantment that flowed as
    the wave,
Where they waited to welcome the murmur
    it gave?

Oh, there's never a shadow where sunshine
    is not,
And never the sunshine without a dark spot;
Yet there's one will be victor, for glory and
    fame,
Without heart to define them, were only a
    name!

LYNN, MASS., February 19, 1868

TO THE SUNDAY SCHOOL CHILDREN

WHO SENT ME THE PICTURE DEPICTIVE OF ISAIAH XI

J ESUS loves you! so does mother:
   Glad thy Eastertide:
Loving God and one another,
    You in Him abide.
Ours through Him who gave you to us, —
   Gentle as the dove,
Fondling e'en the lion furious,
   Leading kine with love.

Father, in Thy great heart hold them
   Ever thus as Thine!
Shield and guide and guard them; and, when
   At some siren shrine
They would lay their pure hearts' off'ring,
   Light with wisdom's ray —
Beacon beams — athwart the weakly,
   Rough or treacherous way.

Temper every trembling footfall,
   Till they gain at last —
Safe in Science, bright with glory —
   Just the way Thou hast:

Then, O tender Love and wisdom,
　Crown the lives thus blest
With the guerdon of Thy bosom,
　Whereon they may rest!

PLEASANT VIEW, CONCORD, N. H., April 3, 1899

HOPE

'T is borne on the zephyr at eventide's
    hour;
It falls on the heart like the dew
    on the flower, —
An infinite essence from tropic to pole,
The promise, the home, and the heaven
    of Soul.

Hope happifies life, at the altar or bower,
And loosens the fetters of pride and of power;
It comes through our tears, as the soft
    summer rain,
To beautify, bless, and make joyful again.

The harp of the minstrel, the treasure of time;
A rainbow of rapture, o'erarching, divine;
The God-given mandate that speaks from
    above, —
No place for earth's idols, but hope thou, and
    love.

TO ETTA

FAIR girl, thy rosebud heart rests
      warm
  Within life's summer bowers!
Nor blasts of winter's angry storm,
  Nor April's changeful showers,

Its leaves have shed or bowed the stem;
  But gracefully it stands —
A gem in beauty's diadem,
  Unplucked by ruthless hands.

Thus may it ripen into bloom,
  Fresh as the fragrant sod,
And yield its beauty and perfume
  An offering pure to God.

Sweet as the poetry of heaven,
  Bright as her evening star,
Be all thy life in music given,
  While beauty fills each bar.

Lynn, Mass., December 8, 1866

NEVERMORE

ARE the dear days ever coming again,
   As sweetly they came of yore,
Singing the olden and dainty re-
     frain,
   Oh, ever and nevermore?

Ever to gladness and never to tears,
   Ever the gross world above;
Never to toiling and never to fears,
   Ever to Truth and to Love?

Can the forever of happiness be
   Outside this ever of pain?
Will the hereafter from suffering free
   The weary of body and brain?

Weary of sobbing, like some tired child
   Over the tears it has shed;
Weary of sowing the wayside and wild,
   Watching the husbandman fled;

Nevermore reaping the harvest we deem,
   Evermore gathering in woe —
Say, are the sheaves and the gladness a
     dream,
   Or to the patient who sow?

LYNN, MASS., September 3, 1871

MEETING OF MY DEPARTED
MOTHER AND HUSBAND

Joy for thee, happy friend! thy bark
        is past
The dangerous sea, and safely
            moored at last —

                    Beyond rough foam.
Soft gales celestial, in sweet music bore —
Spirit emancipate for this far shore —
                Thee to thy home.

" You've traveled long, and far from mortal
        joys,
To Soul's diviner sense, that spurns such toys,
                Brave wrestler, lone.
Now see thy ever-self; Life never fled;
Man is not mortal, never of the dead:
                The dark unknown.

" When hope soared high, and joy was eagle-
        plumed,
Thy pinions drooped; the flesh was weak,
        and doomed
                To pass away.
But faith triumphant round thy death-couch
        shed

Majestic forms; and radiant glory sped
        The dawning day.

" Intensely grand and glorious life's sphere, —
Beyond the shadow, infinite appear
        Life, Love divine, —
Where mortal yearnings come not, sighs
    are stilled,
And home and peace and hearts are found
    and filled,
        Thine, ever thine.

" Bearest thou no tidings from our loved on
    earth,
The toiler tireless for Truth's new birth
        All-unbeguiled?
Our joy is gathered from her parting sigh:
This hour looks on her heart with pitying
    eye, —
        What of my child? "

" When, severed by death's dream, I woke
    to Life,
She deemed I died, and could not know the
    strife
        At first to fill
That waking with a love that steady turns

To God; a hope that ever upward yearns,
              Bowed to His will.

" Years had passed o'er thy broken household
      band,
When angels beckoned me to this bright land,
                With thee to meet.
She that has wept o'er thee, kissed my cold
      brow,
Rears the sad marble to our memory now,
              In lone retreat.

" By the remembrance of her loyal life,
And parting prayer, I only know my wife,
                Thy child, shall come —
Where farewells cloud not o'er our ransomed
      rest —
Hither to reap, with all the crowned and blest,
              Of bliss the sum.

" When Love's rapt sense the heartstrings
      gently sweep
With joy divinely fair, the high and deep,
                To call her home,
She shall mount upward unto purer skies;
We shall be waiting, in what glad surprise,
              Our spirits' own! "

ISLE OF WIGHT

ON RECEIVING A PAINTING OF THE ISLE

Isle of beauty, thou art singing
  To my sense a sweet refrain;
To my busy mem'ry bringing
  Scenes that I would see again.

Chief, the charm of thy reflecting,
  Is the moral that it brings;
Nature, with the mind connecting,
  Gives the artist's fancy wings.

Soul, sublime 'mid human *débris,*
  Paints the limner's work, I ween,
Art and Science, all unweary,
  Lighting up this mortal dream.

Work ill-done within the misty
  Mine of human thoughts, we see
Soon abandoned when the Master
  Crowns life's Cliff for such as we.

Students wise, he maketh now thus
  Those who fish in waters deep,
When the buried Master hails us
  From the shores afar, complete.

Art hath bathed this isthmus-lordling
　　In a beauty strong and meek
As the rock, whose upward tending
　　Points the plane of power to seek.

Isle of beauty, thou art teaching
　　Lessons long and grand, tonight,
To my heart that would be bleaching
　　To thy whiteness, Cliff of Wight.

SPRING

Come to thy bowers, sweet spring,
   And paint the gray, stark trees,
The bud, the leaf and wing —
   Bring with thee brush and breeze.

And soft thy shading lay
   On vale and woodland deep;
With sunshine's lovely ray
   Light o'er the rugged steep.

More softly warm and weave
   The patient, timid grass,
Till heard at silvery eve
   Poor robin's lonely mass.

Bid faithful swallows come
   And build their cozy nests,
Where wind nor storm can numb
   Their downy little breasts.

Come at the sad heart's call,
   To empty summer bowers,
Where still and dead are all
   The vernal songs and flowers.

It may be months or years
  Since joyous spring was there.
O come to clouds and tears
  With light and song and prayer!

JUNE

Whence are thy wooings, gentle
   June?
  Thou hast a naiad's charm;
Thy breezes scent the rose's
    breath;
  Old Time gives thee her palm.
The lark's shrill song doth wake the dawn:
  The eve-bird's forest flute
Gives back some maiden melody,
  Too pure for aught so mute.

The fairy-peopled world of flowers,
  Enraptured by thy spell,
Looks love unto the laughing hours,
  Through woodland, grove, and dell;
And soft thy footstep falls upon
  The verdant grass it weaves;
To melting murmurs ye have stirred
  The timid, trembling leaves.

When sunshine beautifies the shower,
  As smiles through teardrops seen,
Ask of its June, the long-hushed heart,
  What hath the record been?

And thou wilt find that harmonies,
  In which the Soul hath part,
Ne'er perish young, like things of earth,
  In records of the heart.

RONDELET

THE flowers of June
The gates of memory unbar:
     The flowers of June
     Such old-time harmonies *re*tune,
I fain would keep the gates ajar, —
So full of sweet enchantment are
     The flowers of June.
                         — *James T. White*

Who loves not June
Is out of tune
With love and God;
The rose his rival reigns,
The stars reject his pains,
His home the clod!

And yet I trow,
When sweet *rondeau*
Doth play a part,
The curtain drops on June;
Veiled is the modest moon —
Hushed is the heart.

AUTUMN

Quickly earth's jewels disappear;
  The turf, whereon I tread,
Ere autumn blanch another year,
  May rest above my head.

Touched by the finger of decay
  Is every earthly love;
For joy, to shun my weary way,
  Is registered above.

The languid brooklets yield their sighs,
  A requiem o'er the tomb
Of sunny days and cloudless skies,
  Enhancing autumn's gloom.

The wild winds mutter, howl, and moan,
  To scare my woodland walk,
And frightened fancy flees, to roam
  Where ghosts and goblins stalk.

The cricket's sharp, discordant scream
  Fills mortal sense with dread;
More sorrowful it scarce could seem;
  It voices beauty fled.

Yet here, upon this faded sod, —
  O happy hours and fleet, —
When songsters' matin hymns to God
  Are poured in strains so sweet,

My heart unbidden joins rehearse,
  I hope it's better made,
When mingling with the universe,
  Beneath the maple's shade.

Written in girlhood, in a maple grove

ALPHABET AND BAYONET

I<small>F</small> fancy plumes aerial flight,
  Go fix thy restless mind
On learning's lore and wisdom's
    might,
    And live to bless mankind.
The sword is sheathed, 'tis freedom's hour,
  No despot bears misrule,
Where knowledge plants the foot of power
  In our God-blessed free school.

Forth from this fount the streamlets flow,
  That widen in their course.
Hero and sage arise to show
  Science the mighty source,
And laud the land whose talents rock
  The cradle of her power,
And wreaths are twined round Plymouth
    Rock,
  From erudition's bower.

Farther than feet of chamois fall,
  Free as the generous air,
Strains nobler far than clarion call
  Wake freedom's welcome, where

Minerva's silver sandals still
  Are loosed, and not effete;
Where echoes still my day-dreams thrill,
  Woke by her fancied feet.

THE COUNTRY–SEAT

Wild spirit of song, — midst the
    zephyrs at play
In bowers of beauty, — I bend to
    thy lay,
And woo, while I worship in deep sylvan spot,
The Muses' soft echoes to kindle the grot.
Wake chords of my lyre, with musical kiss,
To vibrate and tremble with accents of bliss.

Here morning peers out, from her crimson
    repose,
On proud Prairie Queen and the modest
    Moss-rose;
And vesper reclines — when the dewdrop is
    shed
On the heart of the pink — in its odorous bed;
But Flora has stolen the rainbow and sky,
To sprinkle the flowers with exquisite dye.

Here fame-honored hickory rears his bold
    form,
And bares a brave breast to the lightning
    and storm,

While palm, bay, and laurel, in classical
    glee,
Chase tulip, magnolia, and fragrant fringe-
    tree;
And sturdy horse-chestnut for centuries hath
    given
Its feathery blossom and branches to heaven.

Here is life! Here is youth! Here the poet's
    world-wish, —
Cool waters at play with the gold-gleaming
    fish;
While cactus a mellower glory receives
From light colored softly by blossom and
    leaves;
And nestling alder is whispering low,
In lap of the pear-tree, with musical flow.[1]

Dark sentinel hedgerow is guarding repose,
Midst grotto and songlet and streamlet that
    flows
Where beauty and perfume from buds burst
    away,
And ope their closed cells to the bright,
    laughing day;

[1] An alder growing from the bent branch of a pear-tree.

Yet, dwellers in Eden, earth yields you her
    tear, —
Oft plucked for the banquet, but laid on the
    bier.

Earth's beauty and glory delude as the shrine
Or fount of real joy and of visions divine;
But hope, as the eaglet that spurneth the sod,
May soar above matter, to fasten on God,
And freely adore all His spirit hath made,
Where rapture and radiance and glory ne'er
    fade.

Oh, give me the spot where affection may
    dwell
In sacred communion with home's magic
    spell!
Where flowers of feeling are fragrant and
    fair,
And those we most love find a happiness
    rare;
But clouds are a presage, — they darken my
    lay:
This life is a shadow, and hastens away.

TO ELLEN. " SING ME THAT SONG! "

O SING me that song! My spirit is
     sad,
   Life's pulses move fitful and slow;
A meeting with loved ones in
     dreams I have had,
   Whose robes were as spotless as snow:
A phantom of joy, it fled with the light,
   And left but a parting in air.
My soul is enchained to life's dreary night,
   O sing me, " Sweet hour of prayer "!

Ah, sleep, twin sister of death and of night!
   My thoughts 'neath thy drap'ry still lie.
Alas! that from dreams so boundless and
     bright
   We waken to life's dreary sigh.
Those moments most sweet are fleetest alway,
   For love claspeth earth's raptures not long,
Till darkness and death like mist melt away,
   To rise to a seraph's new song.

O'er ocean or Alps, the stranger who roams
   But gathers a wreath for his bier;
For life hath its music in low minor tones,
   And *man* is the cause of its tear.

But drops of pure nectar our brimming cup
   fill,
  When we walk by that murmuring stream;
Or when, like the thrill of that mountain rill,
  Your songs float in memory's dream.

Sweet spirit of love, at soft eventide
  Wake gently the chords of her lyre,
And whisper of one who sat by her side
  To join with the neighboring choir;
And tell how that heart is silent and sad,
  No melody sweeps o'er its strings!
'Tis breaking alone, but a young heart and
   glad —
Might cheer it, perchance, when she sings.

Lynn, Mass., August 25, 1866

LINES, ON VISITING PINE GROVE CEMETERY

A<small>H</small>, why should the brief bliss of life's
    little day
Grow cold in this spot as the spirit-
    less clay,
And thought be at work with the long-
    buried hours,
And tears be bedewing these fresh-smiling
    flowers!

Ah, wherefore the memory of dear ones
    deemed dead
Should bow thee, as winds bow the tall wil-
    low's head!
Beside you they walk while you weep, and
    but pass
From your sight as the shade o'er the dark
    wavy grass.

The cypress may mourn with her evergreen
    tears,
And, like the blue hyacinth, change not with
    years;
Yea, flowers of feeling may blossom above,
To yield earth the fragrance of goodness and
    love;

So one heart is left me — she breathes in my
    ear,
" I'm living to bless thee; for this are we
    here."
And when this sweet pledge to my lone heart
    was given,
Earth held but this joy, or this happiness
    heaven!

Here the rock and the sea and the tall wav-
    ing pine
Enchant deep the senses, — subduing, sub-
    lime;
Yet stronger than these is the spell that hath
    power
To sweep o'er the heartstrings in memory's
    hour.

Of the past 'tis the talisman, when *we three
met,*
When the star of our friendship arose not to
    set;
And pure as its rising, and bright as the star,
Be its course through our heavens, whether
    near or afar.

LYNN, MASS., August 24, 1865

A VERSE

MOTHER'S NEW YEAR GIFT TO THE LITTLE CHILDREN

FATHER-Mother God,
　　Loving me, —
Guard me when I sleep;
Guide my little feet
　　Up to Thee.

TO THE BIG CHILDREN

Father-Mother good, lovingly
　　Thee I seek, —
　　Patient, meek,
In the way Thou hast, —
Be it slow or fast,
　　Up to Thee.

TRUTH

Beyond the clouds, away
  In the dim distance, lay
  A bright and golden shower
  At sunset's radiant hour, —
Like to the soul's glad immortality,
  Making this life divine,
  Making its waters wine,
Giving the glory that eye cannot see.

  In God there is no night, —
  Truth is eternal light,
  A help forever near;
  For sinless sense is here
In Truth, the Life, the Principle of man.
  Away, then, mortal sense!
  Then, error, get thee hence,
Thy discord ne'er in harmony began!

  Immortal Truth, — since heaven rang,
  The while the glad stars sang
  To hail creation's glorious morn —
  As when this babe was born,
A painless heraldry of Soul, not sense, —
  Shine on our 'wildered way,
  Give God's idea sway,
And sickness, sin, and death are banished
      hence.

LYNN, MASS., April, 1871

" THE LIBERTY BELLS "

THIS is the hour they then foretold —
  When earth, inebriate with crime,
Laughed right to scorn, and guilt,
    grown bold,
  Knelt worshiping at mammon's shrine.

This is the hour! Corruption's band
  Is driven back; and periled right,
Rescued by the "fanatic" hand,
  Spans our broad heaven of light.

Righteousness ne'er — awestruck or dumb —
  Feared for an hour the tyrant's heel!
Injustice to the combat sprang;
  God to the rescue — Liberty, peal!

Joy is in every belfry bell —
  Joy for the captive! Sound it long!
Ye who have wept fourscore can tell
  The holy meaning of their song.

'Tis freedom's birthday — blood-bought
    boon!
  O war-rent flag! O soldier-shroud!
Thine be the glory — nor too soon
  Is heard your "Cry aloud!"

O not too soon is rent the chain
   And charter, trampling right in dust!
Till God is God no longer — ne'er again
   Quench liberty that's just.

LYNN, MASS., February 3, 1865

" MEMENTO "

Respectfully inscribed to my friends in Lynn

I come to thee
O'er the moonlit sea,
When the hoarse wave revisits thy
shore!
When waters shout,
And the stars peep out,
I am with thee in spirit once more.

Then list the moan
Of the billows' foam,
Laving with surges thy silv'ry beach!
Night's dewy eye,
The sea-mew's lone cry,
Witness my presence and utter my speech.

Pleasant a grave
By the " Rock " or wave,
And afar from life's turmoil its goal.
No sculptured lie,
Or hypocrite sigh,
E'er to mock the bright truth of the soul.

Friends, will not ye
Think kindly of me,
In those moments to memory bestowed?
Smile on me yet,
O blue eyes and jet,
Soft as when parting thy sympathy glowed!

March 3, 1867

COMMUNION HYMN

Saw ye my Saviour? Heard ye the
    glad sound?
Felt ye the power of the Word?
'Twas the Truth that made us free,
And was found by you and me
In the life and the love of our Lord.

Mourner, it calls you, — " Come to my
    bosom,
Love wipes your tears all away,
And will lift the shade of gloom,
And for you make radiant room
Midst the glories of one endless day."

Sinner, it calls you, — " Come to this fountain,
Cleanse the foul senses within;
'Tis the Spirit that makes pure,
That exalts thee, and will cure
All thy sorrow and sickness and sin."

Strongest deliverer, friend of the friendless,
Life of all being divine:
Thou the Christ, and not the creed;
Thou the Truth in thought and deed;
Thou the water, the bread, and the wine.

LAUS DEO!

The laying of the corner-stone of The Mother Church

Laus deo, it is done!
    Rolled away from loving heart
    Is a stone.
Lifted higher, we depart,
    Having one.

Laus Deo, — on this rock
(Heaven chiseled squarely good)
    Stands His church, —
God is Love, and understood
    By His flock.

Laus Deo, night star-lit
Slumbers not in God's embrace;
    Be awake;
Like this stone, be in thy place:
    Stand, not sit.

Grave, silent, steadfast stone,
Dirge and song and shoutings low
    In thy heart
Dwell serene, — and sorrow? No,
    It has none,
    Laus Deo!

OUR NATIONAL THANKSGIVING
HYMN

Gᴏᴅ of the rolling year! to Thee we
    raise
A nation's holiest hymn in grateful
    praise!
Plenty and peace abound at Thy behest,
Yet wherefore this Thy love? Thou knowest
    best!

Thou who, impartial, blessings spreadst
    abroad,
Thou wisdom, Love, and Truth, — divinely
    God!
Who giveth joy and tears, conflict and rest,
Teaching us thus of Thee, who knowest best!

Ruler Supreme! to Thee we'll meekly bow,
When we have learned of Truth what Thou
    doest now —
Why from this festive hour some dear lost
    guest
Bears hence its sunlit glow — Thou knowest
    best!

How have our honored dead fought on in
 gloom!
Peace her white wings will spread over their
 tomb;
Why waited their reward, triumph and rest,
Till molds the hero form? Thou knowest
 best!

Shades of our heroes! the Union now is one,
The star whose destiny none may outrun;
Tears of the bleeding slave poured on her
 breast,
When to be wiped away, Thou knowest best!

Thou who in the Christ hallowed its grief, —
O meekest of mourners, while yet the chief, —
Give to the pleading hearts comfort and rest,
In that benediction which knoweth best!

LYNN, MASS., December 7, 1865

SATISFIED

I<small>T</small> matters not what be thy lot,
    So Love doth guide;
For storm or shine, pure peace is
        thine,
    Whate'er betide.

And of these stones, or tyrants' thrones,
    God able is
To raise up seed — in thought and deed —
    To faithful His.

Aye, darkling sense, arise, go hence!
    Our God is good.
False fears are foes — truth tatters those,
    When understood.

Love looseth thee, and lifteth me,
    Ayont hate's thrall:
There Life is light, and wisdom might,
    And God is All.

The centuries break, the earth-bound wake,
    God's glorified!
Who doth His will — His likeness still —
    Is satisfied.

P<small>LEASANT</small> V<small>IEW</small>, C<small>ONCORD</small>, N. H., January, 1900

THE PLIMPTON PRESS · NORWOOD · MASS · U · S · A ·   [4825]